DOCTOR FROWNYFACE'S ☹ SPOOKY WORD LIST TO IMPRESS PEOPLE WITH AT PARTIES, BARS, OR ORGIES*

(*That Is Absolutely Not A Clever Form Of Subliminal Mind Control)

By Doctor Frownyface

with Dusty Trice

READ-☉-VISION

A PUBLISHING COMPANY · LOS ANGELES, CALIFORNIA, U.S.A.

ISBN Paperback: 979-8-9850737-8-2

Library of Congress Control Number: 2025944201

First paperback edition September 9, 2025.

Read-O-Vision LLC, A Publishing Company
6450 Sunset Blvd. #1107, Hollywood, CA 90028
ReadOVision.com

DOCTOR FROWNYFACE'S
SPOOKY
WORD LIST

☹ INTRODUCTION

A NOTE FROM THE DESK OF DOCTOR FROWNYFACE:

Hello. I am a person who knows several words, some of which could be reasonably classified as spooky. This alone fully qualifies me as an expert in spooky words, and you will now place your trust, willingly, in me.

Your quest for a definitive treasury of spooky words begins and ends here. Today. NOW!!!

Congratulations, my friend! You have finally found the mother lode of vile vocabulary words. The singular reference containing all of the words you need to tingle and terrify. That missing spark. That little bit more. The secret sauce! Breathe deep, relax your guts, and rest in peace knowing that you now hold in your hands a whopping 6,500+ spooky words guaranteed to get the blood spilling!

I am quite confident that you'll find MANY situations in which this book of super ICKY words will prove invaluable. Perhaps you're at a party, and someone asks if anyone knows a really spooky vocabulary word. BOOM! You just crack this puppy open, and everyone at THAT party will be in stitches. Too easy!

Not yet convinced? Say you're composing a heartfelt love sonnet about a moonlit graveyard picnic to an unrequited love. You could fumble about, wordlessly, or just whip out this highly useful volume and flip around until you find a spooky word that rhymes with confluence, or worse yet, a spookily poetic word that starts with the letter K. BAM! Your love poem is a hit! You are now engaged to that person over whom you lurked for so long, and you'll be making babies in no time. Proof that being a literate stalker DOES have its benefits!

How about this?! You're trying to write a spooky short story or Hollywood screenplay, but simply can't decide upon the spooky topic(s) about which you wish to write. A serious bummer! Simply thumb through your NEWLY acquired and legitimately purchased copy of "Doctor Frownyface's Spooky Word List...", and all you'll need to do is pick up the royalty checks, because BLAMMO! You found the exact spooky word you needed and now you've got a Pulitzer Prize in literature, a sports car, a condo in Malibu, and everybody simply adores you, coast to coast, kid! And that could be YOU some day very soon, and all because you wisely selected this humble (oh, did I mention that it was humble?) work of spooky nonfiction. What a stroke of genius! You CAD!

Or just use AI or Google all these spooky words yourself on the Internet and pluck along your merry way. No skin off my nose. I simply peddle high-value spooky words, and couldn't care less, dummy.

But do yourself a favor and BUY THIS BOOK and unlock the true secrets and mysteries of the horror literature universe. It is YOUR choice. Don't let me INFLUENCE you. BE the AUTHOR of your own CREATIVE experience. Or else. Just kidding. (But actually NOT kidding.)

Suck it,

-Doctor Frownyface

Read-O-Vision's Spooky
Word Expert, Writ-Large

P.S. I've made it super easy for you to riffle through these pages and know with absolute certainty that you've struck solid spooky gold. Just flip around until the little page number beaker begins to bubble and fizz, and then STOP COLD on any page. How RANDOM is that?! Don't unsettle for less!

DOCTOR FROWNYFACE'S

A

Abandon	Abscess	Acknowledgment
Abandoned	Absinthe	ACME
Abattoir	Absolute	Acne
Aberrant	Absolution	Acolyte
Aberration	Abstain	Acquittal
Abhor	Abstentious	Acre
Abhorrence	Abuse	Acrid
Abhorrent	Abusive	Across
Abnormal	Abysmal	Acrostic
Abnormality	Abyss	Action
Abominable	Accelerator	Activate
Abomination	Accidental	Activated
Abort	Account	Activity
Aborted	Accoutrements	Acumen
Abortion	Accusation	Adamant
About	Accusing	Addict
Above	Ache	Addicted
Abracadabra	Achieve	Addiction
Abrasive	Acid	Adhesive
Abs	Acidic	Adrenaline

Adulterous
Adultery
Adulthood
Advantage
Adventure
Adventures
Advocate
Aeons
Affair
Affear
Affluent
Afraid
Africa
After
Afterlife
Afternoon
Afterward
Afterwards
Afturganga
Again
Against
Aged
Aggressive
Aghast
Agile
Agitated
Agonizing
AI
Aimless
Aimlessly
Ain't
Air

Ajar
Alarm
Alarming
Alarmingly
Alarmism
Alaskan
Alchemist
Alchemy
Alcohol
Alcoholic
Alcoholism
Alcove
Ale
Alien
Alienated
Aliens
Alive
Alkonost
Allah
Allergic
Allergy
Alley
Alleyway
Alligator
Alone
Alpine
Alps
Altar
Alter
Alternative
Aluminum
Always

Amalgam
Amazed
Amazement
Amazing
Amazon
Ambiguous
Ambitious
Ambulance
Ambush
Ambushed
America
American
Amityville
Ammit
Ammonia
Ammut
Amnesia
Amulet
Amusement
Anachronistic
Anagnorisis
Anal
Anansi
Anaphylaxis
Anathema
Ancestor
Ancestral
Anchor
Ancient
Anecdotal
Anesthesia
Angel

SPOOKY WORD LIST

Angels
Anger
Angina
Angry
Angst
Animal
Animalistic
Animated
Ankh
Ankle
Anniversary
Annoying
Anomalist
Anomalistic
Anomalous
Anomaly
Anonymous
Answer
Answers
Ant
Antagonist
Antagonize
Antarctica
Anthropologist
Anthropology
Anthropomorphic
Anthropomorphized
Antibacterial
Antibiotic
Anticipation
Antihistamine
Antimatter

Antique
Antiques
Antiquity
Antler
Ants
Antsy
Anus
Anxiety
Anxious
Anyway
Apartment
Apathy
Ape
Aperture
Apocalypse
Apocalyptic
Apologize
Apothecary
Appall
Appalling
Apparition
Appeal
Appearance
Appendage
Apple
Appointment
Apprehension
Apprehensive
Apprentice
Apron
Apropos
Aquarium

Aquatic
Arachne
Arachnophobia
Arbor
Arc
Arcade
Arch
Archaic
Architecture
Archway
Arctic
Ardent
Arid
Arkham
Arm
Arm-wrestling
Armageddon
Armor
Aroma
Arrant
Arrest
Arrested
Arrow
Arsenic
Arson
Art
Artery
Artifact
Artificial
Artist
Artistic
Artsy

Ash
Ashes
Asia
Aside
Asleep
Asp
Asphalt
Asphyxiate
Aspidochelone
Ass
Assassin
Assassinate
Assassination
Assembly
Asshole
Assiduous
Assignation
Assignment
Assistant
Asthma
Asthmatic
Astonish
Astral
Astrologer
Astrological
Astrologist
Astrology
Astronaut
Astronomer
Astronomy
Asylum
Ate

Atlantic
Atlantis
Atmosphere
Atmospheric
Atoll
Atom
Atomic
Atonement
Atop
Atrocious
Attack
Attacks
Attic
Attitude
Atypical
Audit
Auditory
Aufhocker
Augment
Augmented
Aunt
Auspicious
Australia
Authentic
Authenticated
Automaton
Autopsy
Autumn
Autumnal
Avalanche
Avarice
Avenge

Avenger
Average
Aversion
Aviary
Awake
Awaken
Awakening
Aware
Awareness
Awash
Away
Awe
Awe-inspiring
Awestruck
Awful
Awfully
Awfulness
Awkward
Awning
Axe
Aztec
Azure

B

Babadook
Babies
Baby
Bacillus
Back
Backdraft
Backfire
Background
Backpack
Backside
Backwards
Bacon
Bacteria
Bacterial
Bad
Badass
Badder
Baddie
Baddy
Badger

Badly
Baffled
Bag
Bahamut
Bain
Bait
Baiter
Bake
Bake-kujira
Baked
Baking
Balanced
Balayang
Balcony
Bald
Baleful
Ball
Ballad
Ballerina
Balloon

Balloons
Balls
Ballsack
Balm
Balsamic
Bamboo
Band
Bandage
Bandages
Bandit
Bang
Bangs
Banish
Banished
Banishment
Banjo
Bank
Banks
Banner
Bannister

Banshee
Baphomet
Bar
Bar-B-Que
Barb
Barbarity
Barbed
Barely
Barf
Barfed
Barfing
Barfly
Bargain
Barley
Barn
Barnyard
Baron
Baroness
Baronet
Barrel
Bars
Basan
Base
Basement
Bash
Bashed
Basic
Basilisk
Basket
Bass
Bastard
Bat

Bat-winged
Bath
Bathhouse
Bathophobia
Bathroom
Bathtub
Bats
Batter
Battery
Battle
Battlefield
Bayou
Beach
Beady
Beak
Beaker
Beaks
Beans
Bear
Beard
Bearded
Bearing
Beast
Beastly
Beasts
Beat
Beating
Beautiful
Beclouded
Bed
Bedeviled
Bedroom

Bedspread
Bedtime
Bee
Beef
Beer
Bees
Beetle
Beetlejuice
Beets
Before
Beggar
Begging
Behemoth
Behind
Behinds
Behold
Behoove
Being
Belch
Belching
Belfry
Believe
Believed
Believing
Bell
Bellend
Bellow
Bellowing
Bells
Bellwether
Beloved
Belt

SPOOKY WORD LIST

Bench
Bend
Bending
Benevolent
Bent
Bequest
Berm
Berries
Berry
Berth
Besieged
Best
Bestiary
Bestseller
Betrayal
Betrayed
Better
Between
Beware
Bewitch
Bewitched
Bewitching
Bewitchment
Beyond
Bible
Bicorn
Bicycle
Big
Bigfoot
Bigger
Bike
Biker

Bikini
Bile
Bill
Billow
Bin
Biodiversity
Bioengineered
Biologist
Bird
Birth
Birth-mark
Birthday
Birthmark
Biscuit
Bisection
Bisexual
Bishop
Bit
Bitch
Bitches
Bitchy
Bite
Bits
Bitten
Bitter
Bittersweet
Bizarre
Bizarro
Black
Black-robed
Blackbird
Blackboard

Blackened
Blackguard
Blacklist
Blackmail
Blackmailer
Blackness
Blackout
Blackstone
Blackwood
Blade
Bladed
Blades
Blah
Blair
Blame
Blanch
Bland
Blanket
Blast
Blasting
Blaze
Blazing
Bleach
Bleached
Bleak
Bled
Bleed
Bleeding
Blemish
Blemished
Blight
Blighted

Blind
Blindfold
Blink
Blinking
Blister
Blistered
Blistering
Blitz
Blitzed
Blizzard
Bloat
Bloated
Blob
Block
Blocked
Blocks
Blonde
Blood
Blood-curdling
Bloodbath
Bloodcurdling
bloodcurdling
Bloodiness
Bloodline
Bloodshot
Bloodstain
Bloodstained
Bloodsucker
Bloodthirsty
Bloody
Bloom
Blot

Blotch
Blow
Blower
Blowhole
Blowing
Blowjob
Blown
Bludgeon
Blue
Bluebeard
Blueberry
Bluetooth
Bluff
Blunder
Blunt
Blur
Blurred
Boar
Board
Boarded
Boardwalk
Boat
Boats
Bodies
Bodily
Body
Bog
Bogey
Bogeyman
Boggle
Boggled
Boil

Boiled
Boiling
Bold
Bolt
Bolted
Bomb
Bombed
Bombing
Bone
Bone-chilling
Bone-idle
Bone-setter
Bone-tired
Boned
Bonehead
Boneless
Bones
Bonesaw
Bonetingler
Bonetingling
Boney
Boneyard
Bong
Bonnet
Boo
Boo-boo
Boo-tiful
Boo-tique
Boob
Boobs
Booger
Boogeyman

SPOOKY WORD LIST

Book
Books
Boom
Boor
Boorish
Boot
Booth
Boots
Booze
Boozy
Bordello
Border
Bore
Boring
Born
Borrow
Borrowed
Boss
Botched
Bothersome
Bottle
Bottled
Bottler
Bottom
Bound
Bounty
Bourbon
Bow
Bowels
Bowl
Bowler
Bowling

Bowtie
Box
Boxers
Boxing
Boy
Boys
Bra
Brace
Braces
Brachen
Bracket
Brag
Bragging
Braid
Brain
Brain-eating
Brained
Brains
Brainstorm
Brainwash
Brainwashed
Brainwashing
Braise
Braised
Brakes
Bran
Branches
Brand
Branded
Brandish
Brass
Brassy

Braun
Brave
Braved
Bravo
Brazen
Bread
Break
Breakage
Breakeven
Breakfast
Breaking
Breast
Breasts
Breath
Breathe
Breathtaking
Breed
Breeding
Breeze
Brew
Brewing
Brick
Bridal
Bride
Bridegroom
Bridge
Briefcase
Briefs
Brig
Brilliance
Brimstone
Brisk

Bristle	Buck	Burden
Brittle	Bucked	Burdened
Bro	Bucket	Burdensome
Broach	Bucking	Bureau
Broil	Buckle	Burger
Broke	Bud	Burglar
Broken	Budgeting	Burglary
Bronco	Buffalo	Burgle
Brood	Buffet	Burial
Brooding	Bug	Buried
Broom	Bugaboo	Burn
Broomstick	Bugbear	Burning
Broth	Bugged	Burnt
Brothel	Buggy	Burr
Brother	Bugs	Burrito
Brothers	Building	Burrow
Brought	Bulb	Burst
Brow	Bulge	Bury
Brown	Bulk	Burying
Brownie	Bulky	Bus
Brundlefly	Bull	Bush
Brunette	Bullet	Bushes
Brush	Bullied	Business
Brutal	Bullshit	Businessman
Brutalism	Bully	Businesswoman
Brutalist	Bullying	Bust
Brutalize	Bum	Busted
Brutalized	Bump	Busty
Brute	Bumped	Butcher
Bub	Bumpy	Butchered
Bubble	Bunyip	Butchery
Bubbles	Burble	Butler

Butt
Butte
Butter
Butterfly
Butthole
Button
Buttress
Butts
Buzzard

C

Cabbage
Cabin
Cabinet
Cable
Cackle
Cad
Cadaver
Cafe
Cage
Cain
Cake
Caked
Calcium
Calculating
Calendar
Call
Called
Calling
Callipygian
Callous

Camazotz
Came
Camel
Camp
Campfire
Camping
Can
Canada
Canadian
Cancer
Cancerous
Candelabra
Candies
Candle
Candle-light
Candlestick
Candy
Candyman
Cane
Canine

Cannabis
Canned
Cannibal
Cannibalistic
Cannon
Cannonball
Canoe
Canvas
Cap
Cape
Capsule
Captain
Captivity
Capture
Captured
Captures
Car
Caravan
Carbuncle
Carcass

Carcinogen
Carcinogenic
Card
Cardboard
Cards
Care
Caretaker
Carnage
Carnal
Carnation
Carnival
Carnivorous
Carpet
Cart
Cartilage
Cartoon
Cartridge
Carve
Carved
Carving
Cascade
Case
Cash
Casino
Cask
Casket
Cast
Castaway
Casting
Castle
Casualty
Cat

Cataclysmic
Catacomb
Catastrophic
Catch
Catcher
Catching
Caterpillar
Cathedral
Cats
Cattle
Catwalk
Caught
Cauldron
Caution
Cautious
Cave
Caveman
Cavernous
Caverns
Caviar
Cavity
Celebrity
Celestial
Cell
Cellar
Cellphone
Cellular
Celluloid
Celtic
Cemetery
Cenobites
Censor

Censored
Centaur
Center
Centipede
Centuries
Century
Cerberus
Ceremonial
Cesspool
CGI
Chain
Chained
Chains
Chainsaw
Chair
Chalice
Chalk
Chalky
Challenge
Chamber
Chameleon
Champ
Champagne
Chance
Chandelier
Change
Changeling
Chant
Chanted
Chanting
Chaos
Chapel

SPOOKY WORD LIST

Char
Character
Charcoal
Charger
Charity
Charnel
Charred
Chase
Chasm
Chaste
Chateau
Cheat
Cheating
Cheddar
Cheek
Cheekbone
Cheeky
Cheerleader
Cheese
Cheeseburger
Cheesiness
Cheesy
Chemical
Chemist
Chemistry
Chess
Chest
Chew
Chewed
Chewing
Chickcharney
Chicken

Child
Childhood
Children
Chill
Chilled
Chiller
Chilling
Chimera
Chimney
Chin
China
Chinese
Chip
Chipped
Chips
Chirp
Chocolate
Choice
Choke
Chomp
Chop
Chopped
Chopping
Chortle
Chosen
Christine
Chronos
Chrysalis
Chuck
Chuckle
Chug
Chunk

Chunks
Chunky
Church
Churchyard
CIA
Cider
Cigarette
Cigarillo
Cincture
Cinema
Cineplex
Cinnamon
Cipher
Circle
Circumlocation
Circumspect
Circumstance
Circumstantial
Circus
Citation
Cities
Citrus
City
Civil
Civilized
Claim
Claims
Clairvoyance
Clam
Clan
Clandestine
Clank

Clap
Class
Classic
Claustrophobia
Claw
Clawed
Claws
Clay
Clean
Cleanse
Clear
Cleaver
Cleft
Clench
Clergyman
Clever
Cliché
Clichéd
Client
Cliff
Cliffside
Climb
Clinic
Clipped
Cloaked
Clock
Clone
Close
Close-up
Closed
Closing
Clot

Cloth
Clothes
Cloud
Cloudy
Cloven
Clover
Cloverfield
Clown
Cloying
Club
Clubbed
Clues
Coach
Coagulate
Coal
Coarse
Coat
Cobalt
Cobblestone
Cobra
Cobweb
Cobweb-covered
Cocaine
Cock
Cock-sock
Cockatrice
Cockroach
Cocktail
Codeine
Coffee
Coffin
Coffin-shaped

Coffins
Cognizant
Coil
Coils
Coin
Coins
Cold
Colder
Collapsed
Collar
Collection
Collector
Colloquy
Cologne
Colonel
Colony
Color
Coloring
Columbia
Comb
Combination
Combustible
Comedian
Comedy
Comedy-horror
Comet
Comic
Comical
Coming
Commands
Commonplace
Company

SPOOKY WORD LIST

Compass
Complex
Composite
Comprehension
Compress
Compromise
Comrade
Con
Concert
Concrete
Condemned
Conditioner
Conditions
Cone
Confess
Confessed
Confession
Confessional
Confinement
Conflict
Conform
Confused
Confusion
Congenital
Congestion
Congressman
Congressperson
Congresswoman
Coniferous
Conjure
Conjurer
Conjuring

Conman
Conquer
Conquerer
Conquering
Consanguineous
Conscience
Consciousness
Consequences
Consequential
Conservation
Conservative
Conspiracy
Conspiratorial
Conspire
Constable
Constitution
Constitutional
Constrain
Construction
Consume
Consumed
Contact
Contagion
Contagious
Contaminate
Contaminated
Contender
Contest
Continuous
Control
Convect
Convent

Conversation
Convict
Conviviality
Cook
Cooked
Cookie
Cooking
Cool
Cooler
Cop
Cord
Core
Cork
Corn
Cornbread
Corncob
Cornea
Corner
Cornered
Cornsilk
Cornstalks
Cornucopia
Corny
Corona
Coroner
Corporeal
Corpse
Corpulent
Correction
Corrupt
Corruption
Coruscant

DOCTOR FROWNYFACE'S

Corvid
Cosmic
Cosmopolitan
Costume
Cottage
Coulrophobia
Councilor
Count
Counterfeit
Country
Countryside
Courage
Course
Court
Courtyard
Cousin
Coven
Covered
Covert
Coward
Cowardly
Cowl
Cowlick
Crab
Crackbrain
Cracked
Crackhead
Crackpot
Cradle
Crafted
Crafting
Crafts

Crafty
Cram
Crammed
Cramp
Cranial
Cranium
Crank
Crap
Crash
Crass
Crate
Crave
Craven
Craving
Crawl
Crawlers
Crawlies
Crawling
Crawly
Crazy
Creak
Creaking
Creaky
Cream
Creamy
Creation
Creator
Creature
Creatures
Credits
Creek
Creep

Creepers
Creeping
Creepy
Creepypasta
Cremate
Cremated
Crematorium
Crevice
Cricket
Crime
Criminal
Crimson
Cringe
Cringeworthy
Crinkle
Critter
Croak
Croaked
Crock
Crockery
Crocodile
Crocotta
Crone
Cronenberg
Crook
Crooked
Crops
Cross
Crossbones
Crossed
Crosses
Crossing

SPOOKY WORD LIST

Crotch
Crow
Crowd
Crown
Crucible
Crucified
Crucifix
Crucifixion
Crude
Cruel
Cruelty
Cruise
Crumble
Crumbling
Crunch
Crunched
Crunchy
Crusade
Crush
Crushed
Crusher
Crust
Crusty
Cry
Crying
Cryogenics
Crypt
Cryptozoic
Crystal
Crystals
Cthulhu
Cuddlesome

Cujo
Culprit
Cult
Cultish
Cultists
Cultural
Culture
Cum
Cumrag
Cunning
Cup
Cupboard
Cupidity
Curb
Cure
Curiosity
Curious
Curl
Curling
Curry
Curse
Cursed
Cursing
Curtain
Curtains
Customers
Cut
Cuticle
Cutlery
Cutthroat
Cutting
Cyberpunk

Cyborg
Cyclops
Cynosure
Cytotoxin

D

Dab
Dabbler
Dabbling
Dad
Daddy
Daemon
Dagger
Daily
Dakota
Damage
Damaged
Damn
Damnable
Damned
Damp
Dampened
Dance
Dancer
Dancing
Dandruff

Danger
Dangerous
Dangle
Dangling
Dank
Dare
Dared
Dark
Darken
Darkened
Darkening
Darker
Darkest
Darkling
Darkness
Dash
Dastard
Dastardly
Daughter
Daunt

Daunting
Dawn
Day
Daylight
Daze
Dazed
Dazzle
Dazzled
Deacon
Dead
Deadbolt
Deadly
Deadman
Deaf
Deafening
Dear
Death
Deathblow
Deathlike
Deathly

Deaths
Deathtrap
Deathwatch
Debone
Debt
Debts
Decade
Decades
Decapitation
Decay
Decayed
Decaying
Deceased
Deciduous
Decipher
Deck
Decompose
Decomposing
Decomposition
Decoy
Decrees
Decrepit
Deduce
Deduction
Deed
Deep
Deeply
Deer
Defeat
Defeated
Defecated
Defecating

Defecation
Defect
Defective
Defendant
Defense
Defensive
Deferred
Defile
Defiled
Deflector
Deformed
Deformity
Degree
Dehumanize
Dehydrated
Deity
Deleterious
Deliberate
Delight
Delineating
Delinquents
Delirious
Deliverance
Delivery
Delusional
Delusions
Delve
Delving
Demagogue
Demarkation
Dematerialize
Demented

Demise
Demon
Demoniac
Demonic
Demonology
Demons
Demoralize
Den
Dendrites
Denial
Denied
Dense
Density
Dentist
Dentistry
Deny
Depart
Departed
Departure
Depleted
Deplorable
Depraved
Depravity
Depressed
Depressing
Depression
Depths
Deranged
Derelict
Descended
Descent
Desecrate

SPOOKY WORD LIST

Desecrated
Desecrator
Desert
Deserted
Desideratum
Desire
Desk
Desolate
Desolation
Despair
Despairing
Desperado
Desperate
Desperately
Desperation
Despicable
Despondent
Destiny
Destroy
Destroyed
Destroying
Destruction
Detached
Details
Detective
Detector
Detention
Detergent
Detestable
Devastation
Deviant
Deviate

Deviating
Device
Devil
Devilish
Devilry
Devotees
Devour
Devoured
Devouring
Dewormed
Diabetes
Diabetic
Diabolical
Diagnosis
Dial
Dialed
Dialogue
Diamond
Diaper
Diaphragm
Diarrhea
Diary
Dice
Dick
Dickhead
Diddle
Diddling
Die
Died
Difficult
Difficulty
Diffuse

Dig
Digger
Diggers
Digging
Dilapidated
Dildo
Dilemma
Dill
Dim
Dime
Dimmable
Dimmed
Diner
Ding
Ding-dong
Dingy
Dinky
Dinner
Dinosaur
Dip
Dipped
Dire
Direful
Dirigible
Dirty
Disabled
Disabling
Disagreeable
Disappear
Disappearance
Disappearances
Disappeared

Disaster	Disordered	Dog
Disbelief	Disorientation	Dogged
Discomforting	Disoriented	Dogging
Disconcerting	Dispatched	Dogman
Discord	Disquieting	Doily
Discounted	Dissatisfied	Doink
Discouraging	Dissection	DOJ
Discovered	Dissolve	Doldrums
Discovery	Distant	Doll
Disease	Distasteful	Dollar
Diseased	Distorted	Dolls
Disembark	Distraction	Domain
Disembodied	Distress	Dome
Disembowel	Distressing	Domicile
Disembowelled	Disturb	Dominate
Disembowellment	Disturbances	Dominion
Disgraceful	Disturbed	Donated
Disguise	Disturbing	Donation
Disgust	Ditch	Dong
Disgusting	Dive	Donkey
Disheartening	Diver	Doom
Dishes	Diverged	Doomed
Disheveled	Divergent	Dooming
Disinfect	Divide	Door
Disinterment	Divided	Doorbell
Dislocated	Dividing	Doorknob
Dismal	Divine	Doorstep
Dismay	Dizzy	Doorway
Dismayed	Djinn	Doppelgänger
Dismaying	Dock	Dose
Dismember	Doctor	Doses
Disorder	Dodo	Dot

SPOOKY WORD LIST

Double
Double-headed
Dove
Down
Downspout
Drab
Dracula
Drag
Dragged
Dragging
Dragon
Drain
Drainage
Drainpipe
Drama
Dramatized
Drank
Draped
Drapes
Draught
Draugr
Draw
Drawbridge
Drawer
Drawn
Dread
Dreaded
Dreadful
Dreading
Dreadnought
Dream
Dreamer

Dreaming
Dreamland
Dreariness
Dreary
Dren
Dress
Dribble
Drift
Drifter
Drifting
Driftwood
Drill
Drilled
Drilling
Drink
Drinking
Drip
Dripping
Drippings
Drips
Drive
Drive-in
Drive-In
Driven
Driver
Driving
Drizzle
Drone
Drool
Drooling
Drop
Dropped

Drove
Drown
Drowned
Drowning
Drudge
Drudgery
Drug
Drugged
Druggy
Drugs
Druid
Drum
Drunk
Drunkard
Drunken
Dryad
Dual
Duchess
Duck
Ducks
Dude
Duel
Dueling
Duellists
Dull
Dumb
Dumbfounded
Dumdum
Dummy
Dump
Dumpster
Dune

Dung
Dungeon
Dungeonmaster
Dunked
Dusk
Dusky
Dust
Dustpan
Dusts
Dusty
DVD
Dwarf
Dwell
Dweller
Dwelling
Dwelt
Dying
Dynasty
Dystopia
Dystopian

E

Eagle	Eaves	Educator
Ear	Eavesdrop	Educators
Earache	Eavesdropping	Eek
Eardrum	Ebony	Eel
Earl	Ecantado	Eerie
Earlobe	Eccentric	Effigy
Early	Eccentricity	Egg
Earplugs	Eccentrics	Eggy
Earring	Echo	Ego
Earth	Echoes	Egypt
Earthquake	Eclipse	Egyptian
Easily	Ecstacy	Ejected
East	Ectoplasm	Elbow
Easterly	Ectoplasmic	Elbowed
Eastern	Eczema	Elder
Eat	Edge	Elderly
Eaten	Edging	Eldritch
Eater	Edible	Electric
Eaters	Educated	Electrical
Eating	Education	Electricity

Electrify
Electrocute
Electrocution
Electronic
Electronica
Elemental
Elementals
Elements
Elephant
Elf
Elfin
Elite
Elixir
Elk
Elm
Elopement
Elsewhere
Elusive
Emaciated
Email
Embalm
Embalmed
Embalming
Embarrassing
Ember
Embers
Emblazon
Embolden
Emboldened
Embrace
Embryo
Emergency

Emit
Emotions
Empire
Empty
Emulating
Emulation
Encampment
Encased
Enchanted
Enchanting
Enchantress
Encompassed
Encounter
Encroach
Encrusted
End
Endarken
Ended
Ending
Endocrine
Enemy
Energy
Enervating
Engine
Engineer
Engineered
Engulf
Engulfed
Enigma
Enigmatic
Enlist
Enormous

Ensconce
Ensconced
Enshroud
Enshrouded
Enslave
Enslaved
Ensnare
Entangle
Enter
Enthralling
Entities
Entity
Entomb
Entombed
Entrails
Entrall
Entrance
Entranced
Entrancing
Entrap
Entrapped
Entrench
Entry
Envelope
Envenom
Envenomate
Envenomed
Envious
Environment
Environmental
Envoy
Ephemeral

28

Epidemic
Epidermis
Epigram
Episode
Epitaph
Equality
Equanimity
Equine
Eradicate
Eradication
Erase
Erased
Eraser
Erection
Error
Errors
Escalated
Escape
Escape-artist
Escaped
Escaping
Eschatology
Esoteric
Espresso
Essence
Estate
Estuary
Etched
Etching
Eternal
Eternity
Ether

Ethereal
Euphemism
Euphoria
Europe
European
Evasive
Eve
Evening
Evenings
Evenly
Eventide
Everlasting
Evidence
Evil
Evildoer
Eviscerate
Eviscerated
Evolution
Evolutionary
Example
Exception
Exceptional
Exchange
Excise
Excitable
Excogitate
Execrable
Execution
Executioner
Executions
Exhaust
Exhibit

Exhilarating
Exhilaration
Exhumation
Exhume
Exile
Exiled
Exilement
Existence
Existential
Exit
Exiting
Exorcise
Exorcism
Exorcist
Exorcize
Exoskeleton
Expanding
Expedition
Expensive
Experience
Experiment
Experimental
Experiments
Expire
Expired
Explode
Exploded
Exploit
Exploitation
Explorers
Explosion
Explosive

Express
Expressly
Exquisite
Exsanguination
Exterminate
Extermination
Extinct
Extinguisher
Extract
Extracted
Extraterrestrial
Eyeball
Eyeballs
Eyebrow
Eyed
Eyes

F

Fable	Fakers	Far
Face	Fakir	Far-away
Facebook	Fall	Farm
Facehole	Fallen	Farmer
Faceless	Fallout	Farmhouse
Faces	Fallow	Fart
Facility	Familiar	Farther
Fact	Familiars	Farting
Factory	Family	Farts
Facts	Famine	Fast
Faded	Fan	Fat
Fading	Fandango	Fatal
Fahrenheit	Fang	Fatality
Fail	Fang-tastic	Fate
Failure	Fanged	Father
Faint	Fangirl	Fathom
Fainted	Fangs	Fathoms
Fair	Fanny	Fattened
Fairies	Fantastic	Fattening
Fairy	Fantasy	Fatty

Faucet	Female	Fiendish
Fault	Feminine	Fiendishly
Faun	Femur	Fierce
Favor	Fence	Fiery
Favorite	Fender	Fig
Fay	Fending	Fight
FBI	Fentanyl	Fighting
Fear	Feral	File
Fear-inducing	Ferment	Filet
Feared	Fern	Filled
Fearful	Ferocious	Filling
Fearfulness	Festival	Film
Fearless	Festive	Filmy
Fearmonger	Festivities	Filth
Fearnaught	Fetal	Finale
Fearscape	Fetch	Find
Fearsome	Fetish	Finding
Feast	Fetishist	Finger
Feather	Fetishize	Fingers
Feathers	Fettered	Finish
Feces	Fetus	Finished
Fed	Feud	Fire
Federal	Fever	Fired
Fedora	Fey	Firefighter
Feds	Fiber	Fireman
Fee	Fibers	Fireplace
Feel	Fickle	Firetruck
Feet	Fiction	Firewoman
Feline	Fiddle	Firewood
Fell	Fidgety	Firework
Felon	Field	Firing
Felonious	Fiend	Firmly

SPOOKY WORD LIST

First	Flashing	Float
First-person	Flashlight	Floater
Fish	Flask	Floating
Fisherman	Flatten	Flog
Fitted	Flattened	Flood
Fix	Flatulence	Flooded
Fixed	Flaunt	Flooding
Fixer	Flavor	Floor
Fixing	Flavors	Floorboards
Fizz	Flaw	Flop
Flab	Flawed	Flopped
Flabbergasted	Flax	Flopping
Flabby	Flay	Floppy
Flag	Flayed	Florid
Flagrant	Flayer	Flourish
Flail	Flea	Flower
Flailing	Fleck	Flowers
Flake	Flecks	Flu
Flaked	Fleeing	Fluffy
Flaking	Flesh	Fluid
Flaky	Flesh-eating	Flume
Flambeau	Fleshy	Flung
Flame	Flew	Fluorescent
Flaming	Flick	Flush
Flammable	Flicker	Flushed
Flap	Flickering	Flute
Flapped	Flies	Flutter
Flapper	Flight	Fluttering
Flappy	Fling	Fly
Flare	Flint	Flying
Flash	Flip	Foam
Flashed	Flipped	Foaming

Fog
Foggy
Fold
Folded
Folder
Folding
Folk
Folk-devil
Folklore
Follicles
Follower
Food
Fool
Foolish
Foolishness
Fools
Foot
Footage
Foothills
Forbid
Forbidden
Force
Forced
Forces
Forcing
Forearmed
Foreboding
Foreign
Foreigner
Forest
Foretold
Forewarned

Forfered
Forge
Forgiveness
Forgot
Forgotten
Fork
Forked
Forlorn
Form
Formaldehyde
Former
Formidable
Forms
Formula
Fornicate
Fornication
Fort
Fortification
Fortified
Fortuitous
Fortune
Fortune-telling
Fossil
Fought
Foul
Found
Found-Footage
Fountain
Fox
Foxy
Fracture
Fractured

Fragment
Fragmented
Frail
Frank-N-Furter
Frankenfood
Frankenstein
Fraternity
Fraud
Frayed
Freak
Freaking
Freakish
Freaky
Freefall
Freeze
Freezer
Frenemies
Frenzied
Frenzy
Fresh
Friar
Fried
Friend
Friends
Fright
Frighten
Frightened
Frightener
Frightening
Frightful
Frightsome
Frigid

SPOOKY WORD LIST

Fringe
Frisky
Frisson
Frog
Frog-like
Front
Frost
Froth
Frothing
Frown
Frowny
Frownyface
Frozen
Frugal
Fruit
Fruited
Fruitless
Fry
Fryer
Fuck
Fucked
Fucking
Fucks
Fuckwit
Fuel
Fugitive
Full
Full-bodied
Fumes
Fun
Fun-size
Funeral

Funerary
Funereal
Fungal
Fungous
Fungus
Funhouse
Funk
Funked
Funky
Funny
Fur
Fur-bearing
Furnace
Furnished
Furrow
Further
Fury
Future
Fuzz

36

G

Gagana	Gardener	Gel
Gagged	Gargantuan	Gelatin
Gallbladder	Gargoyle	Gem
Gallery	Garish	Gender-bending
Gallows	Garlic	Gender-bent
Galvanize	Garment	Generation
Galvanized	Gas	Generations
Gamble	Gasconade	Generous
Gambling	Gasconading	Genesis
Game	Gash	Genetics
Gamer	Gasoline	Genganger
Gaming	Gasp	Genie
Gangsta	Gasping	Genitals
Gangster	Gate	Genius
Gangsters	Gated	Gentle
Gap	Gateway	Gentleman
Gaping	Gathering	Gentlemen
Garage	Gaunt	Geometry
Garbage	Gaze	Getaway
Garden	Gears	Ghastly

Ghost
Ghost-ship
Ghostlike
Ghostly
Ghosts
Ghoul
Ghoulish
Giant
Gibbet
Gibbeting
Gift
Gifted
Gigantic
Gilded
Gill
Gill-man
Gilled
Gillman
Gills
Gilt
Gin
Ginger
Girdle
Girl
Giveaway
Gizzard
Glacier
Gladiator
Glamor
Gland
Glashtyn
Glass

Glasses
Glaze
Glazed
Gleeful
Gleefully
Glimpse
Glisten
Glitter
Gloam
Gloaming
Glob
Globe
Globule
Gloom
Gloomy
Glorification
Glorified
Glory
Glove
Glow
Glower
Glowing
Glue
Glued
Glum
Gluten
Glutton
Gluttony
Gnarled
Gnarly
Gnash
Gnashers

Gnat
Gnaw
Gnawed
Gnawing
Gnome
Go-kart
Goatse
Gobble
Goblet
Goblin
God
Godawful
Goddess
Gods
Godzilla
Goggles
Going
Gold
Gold-digging
Golden
Golem
Gone
Goner
Gong
Gonorrhea
Goo
Good
Good-Ol'-Boys
Gooey
Google
Goon
Goonies

SPOOKY WORD LIST

Goop
Goopy
Goose
Goosebump
Gooseflesh
Gore
Gorgon
Gorier
Gorilla
Gory
Gossamer
Gossip
Goth
Gothic
Gourd
Gout
Government
GPS
Grab
Grabbed
Graboids
Graffiti
Grafted
Grail
Grain
Grainy
Grammar
Grammatical
Grand
Grandiloquent
Grandma
Grandpa

Grange
Graphic
Grass
Grassy
Grated
Grater
Grating
Graupel
Grave
Gravel
Graven
Graves
Gravestone
Graveyard
Gravity
Gravy
Gray
Graze
Great
Greater
Greatest
Greed
Greek
Green
Green-eyed
Greenhouse
Greenish
Greens
Greeting
Gremlin
Grenade
Grey

Grievous
Griffin
Grifter
Grill
Grilled
Grim
Grimace
Grime
Grimm
Grimness
Grimoire
Grin
Grinder
Grinding
Grindylow
Grinning
Grip
Gripe
Gripping
Grisliness
Grisly
Gristle
Grit
Gritty
Groan
Groaned
Groaning
Grody
Grog
Groggy
Groin
Groom

Grope
Gross
Grossest
Grotesque
Grotesquerie
Grotesquery
Grotto
Ground
Grout
Grove
Growing
Grudge
Gruesome
Gruesomeness
Grunt
Grunts
Guano
Guard
Guerilla
Guest
Guidance
Guide
Guile
Guileful
Guillotine
Guilt
Guilty
Guise
Guitar
Gulag
Gulch
Gulf

Gum
Gummy
Gun
Gunk
Gunman
Gunpowder
Gurgle
Gurney
Gust
Gusts
Gut-wrenching
Guts
Gutter
Gutterpunk
Guzzle
Gwoemul
Gymnasium
Gypsy

H

Hack	Halloween	Harbinger
Hacked	Halloweenie	Harbor
Hacker	Hallucinating	Hard
Hackers	Hallucination	Hardcore
Hacking	Hallway	Hardened
Hackneyed	Halt	Hardly
Hacksaw	Ham	Hare
Hag	Hamburger	Hark
Hail	Hammer	Harken
Hair	Hammered	Harm
Hair-raising	Hand	Harp
Haircut	Handful	Harpoon
Hairloss	Handle	Harpy
Hairs	Handler	Harrow
Hairstyle	Hands	Harrowing
Hairy	Handsome	Harsh
Hakawai	Hang	Harvest
Half	Hanging	Harvested
Halfback	Hangman	Hash
Hall	Harassing	Hasheesh

Hasp
Hat
Hatable
Hatchet
Hate
Hated
Hating
Hatred
Haul
Haunt
Haunted
Haunters
Haunting
Hauntology
Haven
Hawk
Hay
Hayride
Hazard
Hazardous
Haze
Hazy
Head
Headache
Headless
Headquarters
Headshot
Headstone
Heal
Healed
Healer
Healthy

Heap
Heard
Hearing
Hearse
Heart
Heart-stopping
Heartbreak
Heartburn
Hearth
Heat
Heated
Heath
Heaven
Heavens
Heavy
Heck
Heel
Heft
Height
Heights
Heinous
Heir
Heiress
Hell
Hell-beast
Hell-gate
Hellfire
Hellhound
Hellish
Helmet
Help
Helper

Hemp
Hepatitus
Herd
Herded
Heresy
Hermit
Hero
Herpes
Hesitate
Heteroclite
Heterodox
Heteromorphic
Hewn
Hex
Hidden
Hide
Hideous
Hiding
High
High-strung
Highball
Higher
Highland
Highway
Hikers
Hill
Hillock
Hind
Hindquarters
Hip
Hippie
Hips

SPOOKY WORD LIST

Hiss
Hissing
Historical
History
Hit
Hoarder
Hoax
Hobgoblin
Hobo
Hocus
Hog
Holder
Holdover
Hole
Holes
Hollow
Hollow-point
Holly
Holocaust
Holy
Home-invasion
Homeless
Homophobic
Honest
Honesty
Honey
Honor
Hood
Hoodie
Hoodlum
Hoof
Hook

Hooked
Hooker
Hooligan
Hootch
Hooves
Hop
Hope
Hopeless
Horde
Hordes
Horn
Horn-shaped
Horned
Hornet
Horny
Horrendous
Horrible
Horribleness
Horrid
Horrific
Horrified
Horrifying
Horror
Horror-comedy
Horse
Horseman
Horus
Hose
Hosed
Hoses
Hospital
Hot

Hotdogs
Hotel
Hotter
Houdini
Hound
Hour
Hourglass
House
Hovering
Howl
Howling
Hudhud
Huggable
Hulk
Human
Human-insect
Humanoid
Humanoids
Humble
Humid
Humidity
Humiliating
Humiliation
Humor
Humorous
Humpback
Humungous
Hunchback
Hung
Hunger
Hungry
Hunt

Hunter
Hunters
Huntsman
Hurl
Hurled
Hurricane
Husband
Hush-hush
Husk
Husky
Hybrid
Hyde
Hydra
Hydration
Hyena
Hygiene
Hymn
Hype
Hyper
Hypertension
Hypnotic
Hypnotize
Hypocrite
Hypocrites
Hypodermic
Hypothermia
Hysteria

SPOOKY WORD LIST

I

Ice
Ichabod
Ichor
Icicle
Icky
Icy
Ideas
Identity
Idiosyncratic
Idiot
Idol
Ignite
Ignition
Ignore
Ignored
Iktomi
Ill
Ill-lit
Illegal
Illness

Illuminated
Illusion
Image
Imagination
Imbibe
Imhotep
Imitation
Immeasurable
Immortal
Imp
Impale
Impaled
Impaler
Impassible
Impede
Impeding
Impenetrable
Impish
Implode
Impose

Imposter
Imprisoned
Impromptu
Improv
Improvised
Inanimate
Inca
Incantation
Incarcerated
Incarceration
Incendiary
Incense
Incision
Incisors
Incognito
Incomprehensible
Inconvenient
Incorporeal
Incubate
Incubation

Incubator
Incubus
Indefinite
Indigestible
Indigestion
Individualist
Indolent
Indubitably
Inelegant
Inexplicable
Infantile
Infected
Infection
Inferior
Infernal
Inferno
Infested
Infidel
Infinite
Inflamed
Inflammable
Inflammation
Inflatable
Inflict
Inflicted
Infliction
Influence
Influenza
Information
Infusion
Ingot
Inhabitant

Inhabitants
Inhaler
Inherit
Inheritance
Inherits
Inhumane
Initiate
Initiated
Initiation
Injected
Injection
Injured
Injury
Injustice
Ink
Inky
Inmate
Inmost
Inn
Inner
Innocent
Inordinate
Inquisition
Inquisitor
Insane
Insanity
Inscrutable
Insect
Insecticide
Insects
Insidious
Insomnia

Inspection
Inspire
Inspired
Instant
Institution
Insurance
Intangible
Intelectual
Intellect
Intellectual
Intelligence
Intense
Intensified
Intent
Inter-dimensional
Intercessor
Intercourse
Interment
Internal
Interred
Interrogation
Intertwined
Interval
Intestines
Intimidate
Intimidating
Intimidation
Intoxicated
Intoxication
Intrepid
Intuition
Inundate

SPOOKY WORD LIST

Invaders
Invading
Invented
Invention
Invertebrate
Inverted
Investigate
Investigates
Investigation
Investigator
Invidious
Invincible
Invisibility
Invisible
Invitation
Invocation
Involved
Iridescent
Irksome
IRL
Iron
Ironclad
Ironing
Ironworks
Irradiated
Irrational
Irregularity
Island
Isle
Isolation
It
Itch

Itching
Itchy
Items
Itself
Ivory
Ivy

J

Jab	Japan	Jerking
Jack-o-lantern	Japanese	Jerky
Jackal	Jar	Jest
Jackalope	Jarring	Jester
Jacket	Jars	Jet-black
Jackhammer	Jawbone	Jetstream
Jade	Jaws	Jewel
Jagged	Jazz	Jiggle
Jail	Jazzy	Jiggling
Jailbird	Jealous	Jigsaw
Jailer	Jealousy	Jilted
Jailhouse	Jeep	Jilting
Jalapeño	Jeepers	Jingle
Jam-packed	Jekyll	Jinn
Jambalaya	Jell-O	Jinx
Jambiya	Jellied	Jinxed
Jamboree	Jelly	Jinxing
Jangle	Jellyfish	Jism
Jangling	Jeopardy	Jitters
Janitor	Jerk	Jittery

Jive
Jizz
Job
Jock
Jocks
Jockstrap
Joint
Joints
Joke
Joked
Joker
Jokes
Joking
Jolly
Jolt
Jorōgumo
Jot
Jötnar
Journey
Joust
Jousting
Jovial
Jowl
Joy
Joyless
Jubilee
Judge
Judgement
Jug
Juggernaut
Juggle
Juggled

Juggler
Juggling
Jumbo
Jump
Jumping
Jungle
Junk
Junked
Junky
Jupiter
Justice
Jut
Jute
Juvenile

SPOOKY WORD LIST

K

Kabuki	Kick	Kiss
Kafkaesque	Kicking	Kit
Kaiju	Kidnap	Kitchen
Kappa	Kidnapped	Kleptomaniac
Karloff	Kidney	Knave
Karura	Kill	Knead
Katana	Killed	Knee
Keep	Killer	Kneecap
Keeper	Killing	Knell
Keg	Kiln	Knickknack
Kelp	Kilogram	Knife
Kelpie	Kilt	Knight
Kerosine	Kind	Knob
Ketchup	Kindle	Knobby
Kettle	Kindling	Knobs
Kevlar	Kindness	Knock
Key	Kindred	Knocked
Keyhole	King	Knocker
Keypad	Kink	Knocking
Khaki	Kinky	Knockout

51

Knoll
Knot
Knothole
Knuckle
Knucklehead
Kobold
Kook
Kooky
Kool-aid
Kothoga
Kraken
Krampus
Kratom
Kryptonite
Kudzu
Kush

L

Labia
Laboratory
Laborious
Labyrinth
Labyrinthine
Laced
Lacerate
Lacerating
Laceration
Lacerations
Lackluster
Ladder
Ladle
Lady
Lagoon
Laid
Lain
Lair
Lake
Lamb

Lament
Lamentation
Lamia
Lamp
Lamprey
Lance
Land
Landscape
Landslide
Lane
Language
Languish
Lantern
Larb
Lard
Laser
Last
Lasting
Latch
Late

Lately
Laughed
Laughing
Laughter
Launch
Launched
Laundered
Laundry
Laurels
Lava
Lavellan
Law
Lawbreaker
Laws
Lay
Laying
Laze
Lazy
Lead
Leaden

Leaders	Leviathan	Lily
Leaf	Levitation	Limb
League	Lexicography	Limbless
Leak	Lexicon	Limbo
Leaking	Liar	Limbs
Leaky	Liberation	Limburger
Leap	Librarian	Lime
Leather	Librarians	Limousine
Leatherface	Library	Limp
Leaves	Lice	Limping
Leech	Lich	Line
Leechcraft	Lichen	Linger
Left	Lichgate	Lingering
Leftovers	Lick	Lips
Leg	Licked	Liquid
Legalize	Licking	Liquor
Legalized	Lid	List
Legend	Lie	Listen
Legendary	Lied	Listener
Legs	Lies	Listeners
Lens	Life	Listening
Lenses	Life-size	Listing
Leopard	Lifeform	Lit
Leprechaun	Lifeless	Literary
Less	Ligaments	Little
Lethal	Light	Lived
Lethargic	Lighter	Liver
Lethargy	Lighthouse	Lives
Letter	Lightning	Livestock
Letters	Lights	Living
Leutogi	Lillies	Lizard
Level	Lilliputian	Lizards

SPOOKY WORD LIST

Loathe
Loathing
Loathsome
Lobotomy
Loch
Lock
Lockdown
Locked
Locker
Locking
Lockjaw
Locusts
Lode
Lodge
Lodged
Lodger
Lodgers
Lodging
Loft
Lofty
Log
Logic
Logs
Lollipop
London
Loneliness
Lonesome
Long
Long-dead
Longinus
Loom
Loop

Loopy
Loose
Lord
Lore
Lose
Loser
Loss
Lost
Lot
Lottery
Loudmouthed
Lounge
Lousy
Love
Lovecraftian
Loved
Lovely
Lovers
Low-minded
Lowlife
Lucid
Lucifer
Luck
Lucky
Lugosi
Lugubrious
Lullaby
Lumbar
Lumber
Lumbering
Luminaries
Luminiferous

Luminol
Luminous
Lump
Lumpish
Lumpy
Lunacy
Lunar
Lunatic
Lunch
Lunchbox
Lurch
Lure
Lurid
Lurk
Lurker
Lurking
Lust
Lusty
Luxurious
Luxury
Lycan
Lycanthrope
Lycanthropy
Lying
Lynx

M

Macabre
Macbeth
Macerate
Machete
Machination
Machine
Machinery
Macho
Mad
Madam
Made
Madman
Madness
Maelstrom
Magazine
Magenta
Maggot
Maggots
Maggoty
Magic

Magical
Magician
Magicians
Magistrate
Magma
Magnet
Magnetic
Magnetism
Magnetometers
Maid
Maiden
Mail
Mailed
Mailman
Maim
Maimed
Maiming
Majority
Makara
Make

Maker
Makeup
Malady
Male
Malefactor
Maleficent
Malevolent
Malformation
Malformed
Malice
Malicious
Malign
Malignant
Malleability
Malleable
Mallet
Mammal
Mammary
Mammoth
Man

Mandrake	Mars	Matter
Manes	Marsh	Mattress
Mangle	Marshmallow	Maudlin
Mangler	Marshmellow	Maul
Manhandled	Martyr	Mausoleum
Maniac	Marvelous	Maverick
Manic	Marvels	Maximum
Manipulation	Mash	Maybe
Manly	Mask	Mayhem
Manmade	Masked	Mayor
Manor	Masochism	Maze
Mansion	Masochistic	Maze-like
Mantel	Masquerade	Meadow
Mantle	Mass	Mean
Manuscript	Massacre	Mean-spirited
Map	Massage	Meanie
Marauder	Masses	Meany
Marble	Massive	Meat
Marbleize	Master	Meaty
Marginal	Masterpiece	Mech
Marginalized	Masters	Mechagodzilla
Marijuana	Masterwork	Mechanism
Mark	Masticate	Medical
Marked	Masturbate	Medicated
Marker	Masturbating	Medicine
Market	Mat	Medieval
Marketing	Match	Meditate
Markings	Matchstick	Meditation
Marks	Materialization	Medium
Maroon	Materialize	Medusa
Marooned	Matinee	Meeting
Marrow	Matrimonial	Megalithic

SPOOKY WORD LIST

Melancholy	Methodical	Minotaur
Melody	Mexico	Minuscule
Melt	Mice	Miracle
Melted	Microphone	Mirror
Melting	Microscope	Mirrors
Melty	Microwave	Misbehaving
Member	Middle	Miscommunication
Members	Midget	Miscreant
Memoirs	Midnight	Misfit
Memories	Midwest	Misfits
Memory	Mildew	Mishandled
Menacing	Mile	Miss
Mental	Milieu	Missed
Merciful	Militia	Mist
Mercury	Milk	Mistake
Merfolk	Milky	Mistress
Mermaid	Unalphabetized	Misty
Merman	Mill	Mixed
Mesmeric	Millenia	Moan
Mesmerize	Millipede	Moaning
Mess	Mime	Moat
Message	Mince	Mob
Messenger	Minced	Mobster
Metal	Mind	Mobsters
Metallic	Mind-blowing	Model
Metamorphosing	Mind-blowingly	Modeling
Metamorphosis	Mindless	Modern
Metaphor	Mine	Modest
Metaphysical	Mines	Modesty
Meteoric	Mini	Modicum
Meteorite	Minister	Moist
Methane	Minority	Mold

Moldering	Moonstone	Motel
Mole	Moonstruck	Moth
Molecular	Moonwalk	Mother
Molecule	Moor	Mothman
Molestation	Mooring	Mothra
Molested	Moors	Motion
Molester	Moot	Motivation
Mom	Mop	Motor
Momma	Mopey	Motorcar
Mommy	Mopped	Motorcycle
Money	Moralized	Mound
Monger	Morals	Mount
Mongrel	Morbid	Mountain
Monk	Morgue	Mountain-sized
Monkey	Morning	Mountainous
Monkeys	Moron	Mountains
Monotone	Morph	Mourn
Monotonous	Morphed	Mourned
Monster	Morphine	Mourners
Monsters	Morphing	Mourning
Monstrosity	Mortal	Mouse
Monstrous	Mortalized	Moustache
Month	Mortician	Mouth
Monthly	Mortification	Move
Months	Mortified	Moved
Mood	Mortify	Movement
Moody	Mortis	Movie
Moon	Mortuary	Movies
Moonbeam	Mosquito	Mower
Moonless	Moss	Muck
Moonlight	Mossy	Mucus
Moonlit	Mostly	Mud

SPOOKY WORD LIST

Muddied
Muddy
Mugwump
Mule
Multiply
Mummification
Mummified
Mummy
Murder
Murdered
Murderer
Murderous
Murders
Murk
Murky
Murmur
Muscle
Muscles
Muscular
Museum
Mush
Mushroom
Music
Musk
Musket
Mustard
Musty
Mutant
Mutate
Mutated
Mutation
Mutations

Myrmidons
Mysteries
Mysterious
Mystery
Mystic
Mystical
Mystification
Mystified
Mystify
Myth
Mythological

62

N

Nacht	Nazi	Negativity
Naczehrer	Neanderthal	Negligent
Naga	Near-impenetrable	Neighbor
Nail	Nebula	Nemesis
Nailed	Nebulous	Neon
Nails	Neck	Neophobia
Naked	Necklace	Nephew
Nameless	Necrology	Neptune
Nap	Necromancer	Nerd
Napkin	Necromantic	Nerve-jangling
Narco	Necronomicon	Nerve-wracking
Narcolepsy	Necrophilia	Nervous
Narcotic	Necrophobic	Nest
Narrative	Necropolis	Net
Nasty	Necrosed	Nether
Natural	Necrosis	Nethermost
Nature	Needle	Nethers
Naughty	Needles	Nethersphere
Nay	Nefarious	Netherworld
Nazgûl	Negative	Neti

Network
Neurologist
Neurosis
Neurotoxin
Neutral
Never
Never-ending
New Orleans
Newspaper
Newt
Nice
Nickel
Nidificate
Niece
Night
Night-rising
Night-winged
Nightclub
Nightcrawler
Nightfall
Nightlight
Nightlong
Nightmare
Nightmareless
Nightmarer
Nightmarish
Nightmarishly
Nights
Nightshade
Nighttime
Nightwalker
Nihilism

Nihilist
Ninja
Nipples
Nitrogen
Nixie
No
No-Face
No-good
Nobility
Noble
Nobleman
Noblewoman
Noctambulist
Noctilucent
Nocturnal
Nocturne
Noir
Noisome
Nomads
Nominal
Nonchalant
Nonconformist
Nonexistent
Noodle
Noon
Noonday
Noontime
Noose
Norm
Normal
North
Northern

Norway
Nose
Nosferatu
Nostalgia
Nostril
Nosy
Not
Note
Notorious
Novel
Novelties
Novelty
Nozzle
Nuclear
Nude
Nugget
Nuggle
Null
Nullify
Numb
Numb-nuts
Numbing
Nun
Nunnery
Nurse
Nursery
Nut
Nuts
Nymph
Nympholepsy
NYPD

O

Oak	Observatory	Oddball
Oar	Obsessed	Oddity
Oath	Obsession	Odious
Obelisk	Obsidian	Odyssey
Object	Obstacle	Off-color
Objectification	Obstinate	Off-kilter
Objectionable	Obvious	Offbeat
Objects	Occult	Offender
Obligatory	Occultation	Offensive
Oblique	Occultism	Offer
Obliterated	Occultist	Offering
Obliteration	Occupant	Officials
Oblivion	Occupants	Offspring
Oblivious	Occupied	Ogre
Oblong	Occurence	Ogress
Obnoxious	Ocean	Oil
Obscene	Octave	Oiled
Obscure	October	Oily
Obscured	Octopus	Ointment
Obsequious	Odd	Old

Old-fashioned
Older
Oldest
Olive
Omen
Ominous
Onerous
Onion
Onomatopoeia
Onset
Onslaught
Onyx
Ooky
Ooze
Opal
Opalescent
Opaque
Open
Open-minded
Opened
Opera
Operate
Operated
Operation
Operator
Opium
Opponent
Opposition
Oppressive
Optional
Opus
Oracle

Oral
Orange
Orb
Orbit
Orc
Orchard
Orchestrated
Orchestration
Orchid
Ordeal
Orderlies
Orderly
Organ
Organic
Organism
Organization
Orgasm
Orgasmic
Orgiastic
Orgies
Orgy
Original
Originate
Origins
Ornament
Ornamental
Ornamentation
Ornery
Orphan
Osculator
Osiris
Other

Otherwise
Otherworldliness
Otherworldly
Oubliette
Ouija
Out
Outcast
Outdoors
Outdoorsman
Outhouse
Outlandish
Outlaw
Outpost
Outrage
Outrageous
Outside
Outsider
Outspoken
Outwit
Oval
Ovary
Oven
Over-the-moon
Over-the-top
Overbearing
Overbite
Overblown
Overcast
Overcoat
Overcome
Overdose
Overexcited

SPOOKY WORD LIST

Overhanging
Overhead
Overindulgence
Overlook
Overlooking
Overnight
Overpowered
Overpowering
Oversized
Overturned
Overused
Overwhelming
Owl
Owlish
Owlman
Owned
Owner
Oxygen
Oyster

P

Pacific	Palace	Parachute
Pack	Pale	Parade
Package	Pall	Paradigm
Packed	Pallor	Paradise
Pact	Palm	Paranoia
Pad	Paltry	Paranoid
Paddle	Pan	Paranormal
Paddling	Pancake	Parasite
Pagan	Pandemonium	Parasitic
Pageant	Pane	Parasol
Pail	Panic	Parents
Pain	Panic-stricken	Paris
Pain-faced	Panicky	Park
Pained	Panned	Parlor
Painful	Panning	Parsimonious
Painless	Panther	Part
Paint	Panties	Particle
Painted	Paper	Particular
Painting	Papyrus	Parties
Pair	Par	Partly

69

Partner
Party
Pass
Passage
Passcode
Passenger
Passing
Passion
Passionate
Password
Past
Paste
Pasties
Pastoral
Patch
Path
Patience
Patient
Patriotic
Patrol
Pattern
Pavillion
Paw
Pawn
Pawned
Pazuzu
Peace
Peacock
Peak
Pearl
Peasant
Pebble

Pebble
Peck
Peculiar
Peculiarity
Peddler
Pedigree
Pedophile
Pee
Peeing
Peek
Peel
Peeling
Peep
Pegasus
Pelted
Pelts
Pelvis
Pen
PEN15
Penal
Penalize
Pendulum
Peng
Penis
Penitentiary
Penned
Penny
Pennywise
Pensive
Pentacle
Pentagram
Penultimate

People
Pepper
Peppermint
Perception
Perch
Perfect
Perfidious
Perfume
Perfumed
Peril
Perilous
Period
Peripheral
Perp
Perpetrator
Persecuted
Person
Personal
Perspective
Perspicacious
Perspire
Persuasion
Perturbing
Perusal
Peruse
Perverse
Pervert
Perverted
Pesky
Pessimistic
Pest
Pester

SPOOKY WORD LIST

Pestered	Pick	Pinkie
Pestering	Pickaxe	Pious
Pestiferous	Picked	Pipe
Pestilence	Picking	Pipeline
Pet	Pickle	Pirate
Petrified	Pickled	Piss
Petrify	Picky	Pissing
Petrifying	Picture	Pistol
Phallic	Pie	Piston
Phantasm	Piecemeal	Pit
Phantasmagoria	Pig	Pitch
Phantasmal	Pigeon	Pitchfork
Phantom	Pike	Pitfall
Phantoms	Pile	Pitiful
Pharaoh	Pilfer	Pity
Pharos	Pilfered	Pius
Phases	Pilgrams	Pixie
Phenomena	Pilgrim	Pizza
Philanderer	Pilgrimage	Place
Philosopher	Pill	Plague
Phlegm	Pillage	Plagued
Phobia	Pilloried	Plan
Phobic	Pillow	Planchette
Phoenix	Pimp	Plane
Phone	Pimple	Planes
Photograph	Pin	Planet
Photography	Pinch	Planning
Physical	Pinchers	Plant
Physicality	Pine	Plantation
Physician	Pines	Plasma
Physics	Pinhead	Plaster
Piano	Pink	Plastic

Plate
Plates
Platter
Played
Playground
Playing
Plea
Pleas
Pleasant
Please
Pleasurable
Pleasure
Pledge
Pledged
Plethora
Pliant
Pliers
Plot
Plotting
Plow
Plowed
Plug
Plugged
Plum
Plumed
Plummet
Plunder
Plunderer
Plunge
Plunged
Pluto
Pocket

Pocus
Pod
Poem
Poetry
Point
Pointed
Poison
Poisoned
Poke
Poker
Police
Policeman
Policewoman
Polite
Political
Politics
Pollen
Polluted
Polluter
Pollution
Poltergeist
Poltroon
Polyp
Pomegranate
Pond
Pool
Pooling
Pools
Poop
Pooped
Pooping
Poopy

Poor
Poorly
Pop
Popcorn
Pope
Popped
Poppy
Popsicle
Popular
Population
Porch
Pore
Pores
Pork
Porn
Porno
Pornography
Porous
Portent
Porthole
Portion
Portly
Portrait
Pose
Possessed
Possession
Possessor
Possibilities
Possible
Post
Post-Apocalyptic
Poster

SPOOKY WORD LIST

Posterior
Pot
Potential
Potion
Potted
Pottery
Pound
Pounds
Powder
Power
Powerful
Powerline
Powers
Prairie
Praline
Prank
Prankster
Prawn
Pray
Prayed
Prayer
Precious
Precipice
Precursor
Predator
Predicament
Predicted
Prediction
Predilection
Pregnant
Prehistoric
Premature

Premonition
Prepper
Prepping
Presence
Present
Preserved
President
Press
Pretended
Pretending
Pretense
Preternatural
Prevailing
Prevails
Prey
Price
Prick
Pricked
Prickle
Prickly
Pride
Priest
Priestess
Primal
Primeval
Prince
Princess
Principal
Print
Printed
Prison
Prisoner

Private
Privates
Prize
Prizes
Problem
Proboscis
Procedure
Processed
Produce
Producer
Profane
Professional
Professionals
Professor
Proficuous
Progress
Progressive
Project
Projectile
Projection
Promise
Prompt
Prop
Propaganda
Property
Prophecy
Prophet
Prophetess
Proposal
Prosecution
Prospect
Prostate

Prosthetic
Prostitute
Protagonist
Protect
Provocative
Provoke
Provoked
Provoking
Prowl
Prowler
Proxy
Prude
Prudish
Pry
Psych
Psychic
Psychical
Psycho
Psychological
Psychopath
Psychopathic
Psychotomimetic
Pterodactyl
Public
Pucker
Puddle
Puerile
Pugilism
Pugilistic
Puke
Puking
Pull

Pulp
Pulpy
Pulse
Pulverize
Pump
Pumpkin
Pumpkinhead
Punch
Puncture
Punctured
Punishment
Punk
Pupil
Puppet
Puppetry
Pure
Purgatorial
Purgatory
Purification
Purified
Purifier
Purify
Puritan
Puritanical
Purloined
Purple
Purse
Pursed
Pursue
Pursuit
Pus
Push

Pushed
Pushpin
Pushy
Pussy
Pustule
Putrefaction
Putrid
Putrification
Putrified
Puzzle
Pyramid
Pyre
Pythons

Q

Quack	Quick
Quagmire	Quiet
Quaint	Quill
Quake	Quirky
Quality	Quit
Qualm	Quiver
Quarrel	
Quarter	
Quarterback	
Quartered	
Quaver	
Queen	
Queer	
Quench	
Quenched	
Querulous	
Quest	
Question	
Questioned	
Quetzalcoatl	

76

R

Rabbit	Rail	Rankled
Rabid	Railed	Ransom
Race	Railroad	Rap
Racer	Rain	Rape
Rack	Rainbow	Rapier
Racketeer	Rainy	Rapist
Rad	Raisin	Rapping
Radiant	Ram	Rappings
Radiation	Rambling	Rapscallion
Radical	Ramifications	Rapture
Radio	Rammed	Rarity
Radioactive	Rampage	Rascal
Radiocarbon	Rampaging	Rash
Raft	Rampant	Raspberry
Rag	Ran	Rat
Rage	Rancor	Ratified
Ragged	Rancorous	Ration
Raid	Randy	Rational
Raiders	Range	Rationale
Raiding	Rank	Rats

Rattle	Redcap	Religion
Rattletrap	Redeemed	Relinquish
Raucous	Redneck	REM
Raunchy	Redoubtable	Remains
Raven	Redrum	Remarkable
Raw	Reef	Remarkably
Ray	Reek	Remorse
Rays	Reem	Remote
Razor	Reemed	Render
Read	Refer	Rendered
Reading	Reference	Rendezvous
Readjustment	Reflection	Renovate
Real	Reflections	Renumerative
Realism	Reflector	Repair
Realm	Reformation	Repayment
Reanimated	Refrigeration	Repel
Reaper	Refrigerator	Repellant
Rebel	Refuel	Repellent
Rebellion	Refuse	Report
Reborn	Refused	Repose
Reception	Refusing	Repository
Receptionist	Regeneration	Repress
Reclusive	Regressing	Reprobate
Reconciliation	Regressive	Reproduce
Recovered	Regret	Reptilian
Recovery	Regrets	Repugnance
Recreate	Reign	Repugnant
Recreated	Reincarnation	Repulse
Rectum	Relaxation	Repulsion
Recurring	Release	Repulsive
Red	Relic	Repulsiveness
Red-Haired	Relief	Repurposed

SPOOKY WORD LIST

Requiem
Rescue
Researcher
Resemblance
Residence
Residue
Resin
Resonance
Respect
Respiration
Rest
Restaurant
Rested
Resting
Restless
Restrain
Restrained
Restraint
Restroom
Resurrection
Resurrectionist
Retard
Retarded
Retch
Retention
Retractable
Retribution
Retrofit
Retrograde
Return
Returning
Reunion

Reveal
Revealed
Revealing
Revel
Revelation
Revenant
Revenge
Reviled
Revised
Revisionist
Revival
Revolt
Revolting
Revulsion
Reward
Rhythmic
Rib
Ribald
Ribbed
Ribbon
Ribs
Rich
Richly
Rickety
Rictus
Riddle
Riddled
Riddles
Ride
Rider
Riders
Ridiculed

Ridiculous
Rifle
Right
Rights
Rigid
Rigidity
Rigor
Riled
Rind
Ring
Rinsed
Riot
Riotous
Rip
RIP
Ripe
Ripped
Ripper
Ripple
Risk
Risked
Risky
Rite
Ritual
Ritualistic
Ritzy
Rivals
River
Roach
Road
Roadkill
Roasted

Roasting
Robbers
Robe
Robot
Robotic
Robotics
Rock
Rocket
Rocking
Rocks
Rocky
Rodan
Rogue
Roll
Rolled
Roller
Rolling
Roman
Roof
Room
Roommate
Root
Roots
Rope
Ropes
Rosary
Rose
Rose-bush
Roses
Rot
Rotate
Rotation

Rotator
Rotted
Rotten
Rotting
Rough
Roulette
Rounded
Roundhouse
Route
Row
Rowdy
Rowing
Rubber
Rubbing
Ruby
Rudder
Rude
Rue
Ruffian
Ruffle
Rug
Rugged
Ruin
Ruined
Ruinous
Ruins
Ruled
Ruler
Rum
Rumble
Ruminate
Rumination

Run
Runaway
Runes
Rung
Running
Runny
Rupture
Rural
Russia
Russian
Rust
Rusted
Rusting
Rusty

SPOOKY WORD LIST

S

Sabotage
Sabotaged
Sack
Sacred
Sacrifice
Sacrificial
Sad
Saddened
Saddle
Sadism
Sadistic
Safe
Safety
Sailboat
Saint
Sainthood
Salad
Salamander
Sale
Salem

Salesman
Saliva
Salmon
Salon
Salt
Salted
Salvage
Samhain
Sample
Sanctuary
Sand
Sandman
Sandwich
Sandworm
Sandy
Sanguine
Sanity
Sank
Sap
Sapphire

Saratan
Sarcasm
Sarcastic
Sarcastically
Sarcophagus
Sash
Sasquatch
Satan
Satanic
Satellite
Satiating
Satisfaction
Satisfied
Saturn
Satyr
Sauce
Saucer
Saucy
Sausage
Savage

Savagery
Saved
Savior
Savvy
Saw
Saxicolous
Saxophone
Scab
Scabbed
Scalawag
Scald
Scalded
Scallywag
Scalp
Scalpel
Scam
Scammed
Scammer
Scamp
Scandal
Scandalous
Scapegoat
Scapegrace
Scar
Scarabs
Scare
Scarecrow
Scared
Scaredy
Scaremonger
Scarf
Scariest

Scaring
Scarlet
Scarred
Scarring
Scars
Scat
Scatological
Scepter
Scheming
Schlock
School
Science
Sciences
Scientist
Scimitar
Scissors
Sconce
Scorch
Scorched
Scorching
Scorpion
Scoundrel
Scourge
Scramble
Scrambled
Scrap
Scrape
Scraping
Scratch
Scratched
Scratching
Scream

Screaming
Screams
Screech
Screen
Screening
Screw
Screwball
Screwed
Screwy
Scroll
Scrunch
Scrunchie
Scuba
Scuffed
Scuzzy
Scythe
Sea
Seagull
Seal
Seam
Séance
Sear
Search
Searcher
Seas
Seashore
Seaside
Seaweed
Secluded
Second
Secret
Secretary

83

Secreted
Secrets
Securities
Security
Seed
Seedling
Seeping
Seer
Self-driving
Self-sufficient
Selket
Selkie
Semaglutide
Semen
Semi-dark
Senator
Senile
Senior
Sense
Senses
Sensitive
Sensual
Sensuality
Sensuous
Sentenced
Sentient
Separate
Septum
Sepulcher
Sepulchral
Sequin
Serial

Serpent
Servant
Sessions
Settlement
Settler
Severe
Severed
Sew
Sewage
Sewer
Sex
Sexism
Sexton
Sexual
Sexuality
Sexualized
Sexy
Shade
Shaded
Shades
Shadow
Shadows
Shadowy
Shady
Shaft
Shake
Shaken
Shaker
Shaking
Shaky
Shakycam
Shambles

Shambling
Shame
Shameless
Shampoo
Shape
Shape-shifter
Shapeless
Shard
Share
Shared
Sharing
Shark
Sharktopus
Sharp
Sharpened
Sharpest
Shart
Shat
Shave
Shaved
Shaving
Shed
Sheep
Shell
Shellfish
Shelling
Shelob
Shelter
Shelves
Shepard
Shift
Shifted

SPOOKY WORD LIST

Shifting
Shiftless
Shifty
Shin
Shine
Shining
Shins
Shiny
Ship
Shipwreck
Shit
Shite
Shitless
Shitty
Shiver
Shivery
Shizzle
Shoals
Shock
Shocked
Shocking
Shockproof
Shoe
Shoelaces
Shoes
Shoot
Shooter
Shooting
Shootings
Shore
Short
Shorts

Shot
Shotgun
Shots
Shout
Shove
Shoved
Shovel
Shoving
Show
Shower
Showers
Shrank
Shred
Shredded
Shriek
Shrieking
Shrimp
Shrine
Shrinking
Shriveled
Shroud
Shrouded
Shrunk
Shudder
Shuddering
Shuddersome
Shuddery
Shun
Shunned
Shut
Shutter
Shutters

Shy
Shyness
Sick
Sickening
Sickness
Sidekick
Sideshow
Sidewalk
Siesta
Sight
Sign
Signal
Signals
Silence
Silent
Silicone
Silly
Silver
Simian
Simple
Simpleton
Simulation
Sin
Sinew
Sinewy
Singe
Singing
Sings
Singular
Singularity
Sinister
Sink

Sinking
Sinner
Sinuses
Sip
Siphon
Siren
Sirens
Sister
Sisterhood
Sisters
Sit
Sitting
Situation
Skate
Skating
Skeksis
Skeletal
Skeleton
Skewer
Ski
Skid
Skidding
Skies
Skiing
Skill
Skills
Skim
Skin
Skin-walker
Skinned
Skinny
Skittish

Skulk
Skulking
Skull
Skulls
Skunk
Skunky
Sky
Skyscraper
Skyward
Slab
Slain
Slam
Slammed
Slander
Slanderous
Slap
Slapped
Slash
Slashed
Slasher
Slate
Slated
Slaughter
Slave
Slaw
Slay
Slayer
Slaying
Sleaze
Sleazeball
Sleazy
Sled

Sleep
Sleep-walker
Sleep-walking
Sleeper
Sleeping
Sleepless
Sleepy
Sleet
Sleeve
Sleigh
Slender
Slice
Slime
Slimed
Slimy
Sling
Slinking
Slinky
Slip
Slit
Sliver
Slop
Sloppy
Slosh
Sloth
Slothful
Sloven
Slow
Slowly
Slumber
Slung
Slur

SPOOKY WORD LIST

Slurp	Snaking	Society
Slut	Snap	Sock
Sly	Snapped	Socket
Smarmy	Snappy	Socks
Smash	Snare	Soda
Smashed	Snared	Soft
Smasher	Snarge	Softened
Smashing	Snark	Solar
Smaug	Snarky	Soldier
Smeared	Snatch	Solicitor
Smell	Snatcher	Solidify
Smile	Snatches	Solution
Smirk	Sneak	Somber
Smog	Sneaker	Sombre
Smoggy	Sneeze	Something
Smoke	Snide	Son
Smoked	Snipe	Song
Smoker	Snitch	Sonnet
Smoking	Snooker	Soon
Smolder	Snoot	Soot
Smoldering	Snore	Sooty
Smother	Snoring	Sorcerer
Smudge	Snort	Sorcery
Smuggled	Snot	Sordid
Smut	Snout	Sordidness
Smutty	Snow	Sorority
Snag	Snowier	Sorrow
Snail	Soap	Sorrowful
Snake	Sob	Sorrows
Snaked	Sobbed	Soul
Snakes	Sobbing	Souls
Snakeskin	Social	Soup

Soupy	Spectral	Spiralling
Sour	Spectre	Spirit
South	Speculum	Spirited
Southern	Speech	Spirits
Space	Speeding	Spit
Spaceship	Spell	Spittle
Spade	Spellbound	Splash
Spake	Spew	Splat
Spank	Spheres	Splatter
Spar	Sphinx	Splatter-punk
Spare	Spice	Splattered
Spark	Spiced	Spleen
Sparked	Spicy	Splendiferous
Sparkle	Spider	Spliced
Sparkles	Spiders	Split
Sparkling	Spiderweb	Splitting
Sparkly	Spike	Spoil
Spastic	Spiked	Spoiled
Spat	Spikes	Spoke
Spatter	Spill	Spokesperson
Spawn	Spilled	Sponge
Spawned	Spin	Spoof
Speaking	Spinach	Spook
Spear	Spindle	Spookbinding
Special	Spindly	Spookbound
Specimen	Spine	Spooked
Specimens	Spine-chilling	Spookiest
Speck	Spine-tingling	Spookified
Speckled	Spineless	Spooky
Spectacle	Spinning	Spool
Spectacles	Spiral	Spoon
Specter	Spiraling	Spooning

Spore	Squire	Stapler
Spot	Squirreled	Staples
Spotlight	Squirt	Star
Spotted	Squish	Starless
Spout	Squishy	Starry
Sprain	Stab	Startle
Sprawl	Stabbed	Startling
Sprawling	Staff	Starve
Spray	Stage	Statement
Sprayer	Stagnant	Station
Spread	Stain	Statue
Spreader	Stained	Status
Spreading	Staining	Stay
Sprinkle	Stair	Stay-Puft
Sprite	Staircase	Staying
Spritz	Stairs	STD
Sprout	Stairway	Steak
Spun	Stake	Steal
Spur	Staked	Stealth
Sputter	Stakes	Stealthy
Sputum	Stalactite	Steam
Spy	Stalagmite	Steamed
Spying	Stale	Stench
Squad	Stalk	Step
Squalid	Stalked	Stepped
Square	Stalker	Stiches
Squared	Stalking	Sticker
Squeak	Stalls	Stickers
Squeal	Standard	Sticking
Squeeze	Stank	Sticks
Squelch	Stanza	Sticky
Squid	Stapled	Stiff

SPOOKY WORD LIST

Stiffy
Still
Stillborn
Stimulates
Sting
Stinger
Stink
Stinker
Stinking
Stinky
Stitch
Stitches
Stock
Stockade
Stockbroker
Stocks
Stole
Stolen
Stomach
Stone
Stoned
Stonehenge
Stoning
Stony
Stop
Stoplight
Stopped
Storage
Storm
Stormy
Story
Stove

Stovepipe
Strain
Strained
Strait-jacket
Strand
Stranded
Strange
Stranger
Strangled
Strangling
Strap
Strappado
Strapped
Straps
Strategically
Strategy
Street
Streetlight
Stress
Stressed
Stressful
Stretch
Stretched
Stricken
Strike
Striking
String
Strip
Striped
Stripped
Stripper
Strix

Strolling
Struck
Structured
Struggle
Stubborn
Stuck
Stud
Student
Studio
Stuff
Stumble
Stumblebum
Stump
Stun
Stunk
Stunned
Stunner
Stunning
Stunt
Stupid
Stutter
Sty
Stygian
Style
Suave
Sub-freezing
Subdued
Subject
Sublime
Subliminal
Submarine
Submission

Subterranean
Subway
Succinct
Succubus
Succumb
Succumbing
Suck
Suction
Suffering
Suffocate
Suffocating
Suffocation
Sugar
Suggestive
Suicidal
Suicide
Suit
Suitable
Suitcase
Suite
Suitor
Sulfur
Sully
Sultana
Summer
Summit
Summon
Summoned
Summoning
Sun
Sunglasses
Sunk

Sunken
Sunlight
Sunrise
Sunset
Super-virus
Supercilious
Superiority
Supernatural
Superstition
Superstitious
Supreme
Surf
Surfing
Surgery
Surgical
Surprise
Surprised
Surreal
Surrealism
Surrender
Surreptitious
Surrounded
Survival
Survive
Survived
Surviving
Survivor
Survivors
Susceptible
Suspense
Suspicious
Swagger

Swallow
Swallowed
Swamp
Swapping
Sway
Swear
Sweat
Sweaty
Sweep
Sweetheart
Sweets
Swim
Swimmer
Swimming
Swine
Swing
Swinging
Swinish
Swipe
Swiped
Swirl
Swirly
Swish
Switch
Sword
Swung
Symphony
Syndrome
Synergy
Syphilis
Syringe
System

92

T

Tabernacle
Table
Taboo
Taffy
Tail
Tailor
Taint
Tale
Talisman
Talk
Tall
Tallow
Talon
Talons
Tame
Tangent
Tangie
Tangle
Tangled
Tangling

Tango
Tank
Tap
Tape
Tapestried
Tapestry
Tapping
Tar
Tarantula
Target
Targeted
Tariff
Tarnish
Tarnished
Tarot
Tarp
Tassel
Taste
Tasteless
Tasting

Tasty
Tattoo
Tattooed
Taunt
Taunting
Taxed
Taxes
Taxi
Taxidermist
Taxidermy
Tea
Teacher
Teak
Tear
Tearjerking
Tears
Tease
Teaser
Tech
Techniques

Technological
Teen
Teens
Teeth
Telekinesis
Telekinetic
Telepathic
Telephone
Television
Templar
Templars
Temple
Temporal
Temporary
Temptation
Tempter
Tenacious
Tenderfoot
Tendons
Tenebrosity
Tenebrous
Tense
Tension
Tensions
Tent
Tentacle
Tepid
Terminate
Terminator
Terminology
Terrace
Terrible

Terribly
Terrified
Terrifier
Terrifying
Terror
Terrorist
Terrorize
Terrorized
Terrors
Tesla
Tested
Testicles
Testimony
Texas
Thanatophobia
Thaw
Theater
Them
Theme
Theory
Therapist
Thermal
Thermos
They
Thick
Thief
Thieves
Thing
Think
Thinker
Thinking
Thirsty

Thirteen
Thirteenth
Thought
Thoughts
Thousand
Thrash
Thrashing
Threads
Threat
Threatening
Threats
Threesome
Thrill
Thriller
Thrillers
Throat
Throaty
Throbbing
Throne
Throng
Throttle
Through
Throw
Throwback
Throwing
Thrown
Thrust
Thruster
Thud
Thug
Thumb
Thump

SPOOKY WORD LIST

Thunder
Thunderbird
Thunderbolt
Tick
Tick-tock
Ticket
Tickets
Ticking
Tide
Tides
Tie
Tied
Tiger
Tight
Tiki
TikTok
Tile
Timber
Time
Timeless
Timely
Timepiece
Times
Timid
Timidity
Timorous
Tincture
Ting
Tingle
Tingled
Tingling
Tinkle

Tip
Tips
Tire
Tired
Tiresome
Tiring
Tissue
Titan
Titanic
Tits
Titties
Titular
Tjinimin
Toad
Toast
Toasted
Toe
Toffee
Toil
Toilet
Toilsome
Token
Tokyo
Toll
Tollbooth
Tomato
Tomb
Tombstone
Tome
Ton
Tone
Tongue

Tongues
Tons
Tool
Tooth
Toothache
Toothsome
Toothy
Top
Topical
Topple
Toppled
Torch
Torched
Torment
Tormented
Torn
Tornado
Torso
Tortoise
Tortoise-shell
Torture
Tortured
Touch
Tough
Towel
Tower
Towering
Town
Toxic
Toxin
Toy
Toying

Toys
Tractor
Trading
Tradition
Traditional
Traffic
Tragedy
Tragic
Trail
Trailer
Train
Trained
Training
Traitor
Tramp
Tramping
Trampled
Trance
Transcend
Transcendence
Transcendent
Transcendental
Transexual
Transfer
Transformation
Transformed
Transgress
Transgressive
Transgressor
Transition
Translucent
Transmigration

Transmission
Transmissions
Transmogrify
Transparent
Transport
Transported
Transvestite
Transylvania
Transylvanian
Trap
Trapped
Trapper
Trash
Trashed
Trashy
Trauma
Traumatic
Tray
Treacherous
Treachery
Treadmill
Treasure
Treat
Treatment
Treaty
Treble
Tree
Trees
Trek
Tremble
Trembling
Tremor

Trench
Trenches
Trepidation
Trespass
Trespasser
Trespassing
Trial
Trials
Triangle
Trick
Trick-or-treat
Trickle
Tricks
Trickster
Tricky
Trident
Tried
Trinket
Trip
Tripe
Triptych
Triskaidekaphobia
Triumph
Trod
Troll
Troop
Trophy
Tropical
Trouble
Troubling
Truck
Truck-sized

96

SPOOKY WORD LIST

Trump
Trumped
Trumpet
Trundle
Trunk
Truth
Trying
Tryst
TSA
Tsuchigumo
Tsunami
Tub
Tube
Tubing
Tummy
Tumor
Tunnel
Tunnels
Turd
Turducken
Turkey
Turmoil
Turnip
Turret
Turtle
Tusk
Tussle
Tweet
Tweezers
Twilight
Twine
Twins

Twirl
Twist
Twisted
Twitter
Two-faced
Twosome
Tyrannosaurus

U

Uglier	Unclean	Undertaker
Ugly	Uncles	Undertow
Ukelele	Uncoiled	Underwater
Ulcer	Uncommon	Underwear
Ulceration	Unconscious	Undress
Ultimate	Unconventional	Undressed
Umbrella	Uncool	Unearth
Unafraid	Uncouth	Unearthly
Unbearable	Uncover	Unencumbered
Unbelievable	Uncultured	Unethical
Unbolted	Uncustomary	Unexpected
Unburied	Undead	Unexpectedly
Uncanny	Undefined	Unexplained
Uncanonized	Under-the-table	Unfathomable
Uncertain	Undercarriage	Unfeared
Uncharted	Undercover	Unfeeling
Unchecked	Underground	Unfinished
Uncivilized	Underhand	Unfold
Unclaimed	Underhanded	Unfortunate
Uncle	Underneath	Unfriend

DOCTOR FROWNYFACE'S

Unfriendly
Unfulfilled
Unfunny
Unfurl
Unfurled
Unfurnished
Unhappiness
Unhappy
Unhealthy
Unheard
Unholy
Unibomber
Unibrow
Unicorn
Unicycle
Uniform
Unilateral
Union
Universe
Unknowability
Unknown
Unleashed
Unleashes
Unlucky
Unmasked
Unmitigated
Unnameable
Unnamed
Unnatural
Unnerving
Unoriginality
Unorthodox

Unparagoned
Unpatriotic
Unpleasant
Unprovoked
Unqualified
Unreal
Unrecognizable
Unrefined
Unrelated
Unreliable
Unrequited
Unrest
Unrestful
Unsafe
Unsatisfied
Unscrew
Unseemly
Unseen
Unsettled
Unsettling
Unsolved
Unsophisticated
Unspeakable
Unspool
Unstable
Untenanted
Untouchable
Unveiled
Unwell
Unwieldy
Unwind
Unwinding

Unzip
Upgraded
Upgrades
Upon
Upper
Upright
Upset
Upsetting
Uranus
Urban
Urinal
Urination
Urine
Urn
Urologist
Use
Used
Usher
Usual
UTI
Utter

V

Vacant	Vanish	Veil
Vacillate	Vanished	Veiled
Vacuum	Vanishing	Vein
Vagabond	Vanities	Veiny
Vagina	Vanity	Velcro
Vain	Vapid	Velvet
Valhalla	Vapor	Veneer
Valkyrie	Vaporize	Venetian
Valley	Vaporized	Vengeance
Valueless	Vaporizer	Vengeful
Vampira	Variet	Venison
Vampire	Varnish	Venom
Vampirella	Vat	Venomous
Vampiress	Vault	Ventilated
Vampiric	Vaulted	Ventilation
Vampirism	Vaulting	Venture
Vanara	Veal	Venus
Vandal	Vegetables	Vermin
Vandalism	Vegetal	Vertebra
Vandals	Vegetation	Vertebrae

Vesper
Vessel
Vest
Vestige
Vetala
Vexing
Vial
Vibe
Victim
Victimize
Video
Videogame
Videogamer
Videotape
Videotaped
Vienna
Vigil
Vile
Villa
Village
Villain
Villainess
Vine
Vinegar
Vines
Vineyard
Vintage
Violation
Violence
Violent
Violin
Viper

Viral
Virgin
Virginity
Virtual
Virtue
Virtuoso
Virus
Visceral
Vision
Visions
Visitant
Visitation
Visitor
Vitamins
Vivacious
Vivid
Vivisection
Vocation
Vodka
Voice
Voices
Void
Volcanic
Volcano
Vole
Volume
Vomit
Vomited
Vomiting
Voodoo
Voracious
Vortex

Vortices
Vow
Voyage
Vulgar
Vulnerable
Vulture

W

Wacky	Walls	Wartime
Waffle	Waltz	Wash
Wager	Wand	Washed
Wagon	Wanded	Washington
Waif	Wander	Wasp
Wail	Wandering	Waste
Wailing	Wanderlust	Wasted
Waining	Waned	Wasteland
Wait	Waning	Watch
Waited	War	Watcher
Waiting	Wardrobe	Watchers
Wake	Warfare	Watching
Wakes	Warlock	Watchman
Waking	Warm	Water
Walk	Warmth	Watered
Walker	Warning	Waterfall
Walking	Warp	Waterpipe
Wall	Warped	Watery
Walled	Warrior	Wave
Wallpaper	Wart	Waver

Wavering	Wench	Whopper
Waves	Wendigo	Whowie
Wax	Werehyena	Wicca
Waxen	Werejaguar	Wick
Way-out	Werewolf	Wicked
Wayfarers	Werewolves	Wickedest
Wealthy	West	Wickedness
Weapon	Westerly	Widow
Weaponry	Western	Widower
Weapons	Wet	Wiedergänger
Wearisome	Wetting	Wife
Weaver	Whack	Wig
Weaving	Whale	Wiggled
Web	What	Wiggles
Webbed	Wheat	Wiggling
Website	Wheel	Wild
Wedding	Wheelchair	Wilderness
Weed	Wheelhouse	Will
Weeds	Whip	Will-o'-the-wisp
Weekday	Whipped	Willow
Weekend	Whirling	Willows
Weekly	Whirlwind	Wily
Weep	Whiskey	Wimp
Weeping	Whisper	Wince
Weigh	Whispering	Winced
Weight	Whistle	Winch
Weighty	White	Winchester
Weiner	Whiteboard	Wincing
Weird	Whitened	Wind
Weirdest	Whiteout	Winding
Weirdo	Whiz	Windmill
Well	Whomp	Window

SPOOKY WORD LIST

Winds
Windstorm
Wine
Winebibber
Wing
Winged
Winter
Wipe
Wiped
Wiping
Wire
Wire-haired
Wireless
Wisdom
Wise
Wish
Wishful
Wishing
Wisp
Wit
Witch
Witch-hazel
Witch-hunt
Witchcraft
Witches
Witchfinder
Witching
Wither
Withered
Without
Witness
Wits

Witty
Wizard
Wizardry
Wobble
Woke
Wolf
Wolfbane
Wolfhound
Wolfman
Wolfsbane
Wolpertinger
Wolves
Woman
Wonder
Wonderful
Wonderment
Wonders
Wood
Wooden
Woodland
Woods
Woodsman
Woodstone
Wool
Woolen
Woozier
Woozy
Work
Workplace
World
Worm
Worm-casts

Wormed
Wormhole
Wormwood
Worrisome
Worry
Worrying
Worse
Worshiping
Worshipping
Worst
Wound
Wounded
Wow
Wowza
Wraith
Wraithlike
Wrapped
Wrapping
Wrappings
Wreath
Wrench
Wretch
Wrinkle
Wrinkly
Wrist
Writer
Writers
Writing
Written
Wrong
Wrongdoer
Wrought

<u>X</u>

X-ray
X-rays
Xanthic
Xebec
Xenobiotics
Xenogenesis
Xenolith
Xenomorph
Xenophobic
Xeric

DOCTOR FROWNYFACE'S

Y

Yacht
Yak
Yarn
Yawn
Year
Yearbook
Yearly
Yearn
Yeast
Yell
Yelling
Yellow
Yes
Yet
Yeti
Yikes
Yipes
Yo-yo
Yogurt
Yoinks

Young
Youth
Yowie
Yowl
Yowling
Yuck
Yucky
Yummy

DOCTOR FROWNYFACE'S

Z

Zany
Zap
Zapped
Zaratan
Zealot
Zealotry
Zealous
Zebra
Zeitgeist
Zen
Zenith
Zephyr
Zeppelin
Zero
Zest
Zig-zag
Zilch
Zinger
Zipline
Ziplining

Zipper
Zippy
Zodiac
Zombie
Zombified
Zombify
Zone
Zoom
Zydeco

BOOK
OVER.

FUCK
OFF.

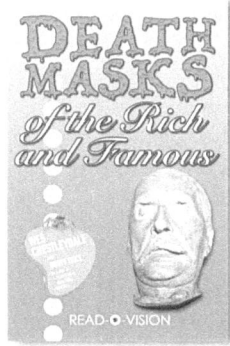